DEAR MOM

A WWII MEMOIR

RJ VAN DRESS

DEAR MOM

A WWII MEMOIR

RJ VAN DRESS

with an introduction by
Stephanie Pope, mythopoetry.com

This is an account of my time spent as a soldier during WWII in a combat infantry machine gun squad [Company D, 17th Infantry Regiment, Seventh Division], in what is now known as one of the bloodiest battles of the Pacific and the last battle of WWII, The Battle for Okinawa.

waterforestpressbooks.com

Death is absolute and without memorial
      —Wallace Stevens, *The Death of a Soldier*

Death is not an event in life: we do not live to experience death. If we take eternity to mean not infinite temporal duration but timelessness, then eternal life belongs to those who live in the present. Our life has no end in the way in which our visual field has no limits.
      —Ludwig Wittgenstein, *Tractatus Logico-Philosophicus*

*In memory of my dear mother who
sent four sons to serve our country in World War II. And,
to all mothers who, like she, could only wait and pray.*

AWARDS

Combat Infantry Man's Badge
The Bronze Star
Numerous Ribbons With One Battle Star
Corporal Stripes
Three (3) Gold Overseas Service Bars

CONTENTS

Acknowledgements

I express appreciation to The Canton Repository for permission to use in the foreword of my memoir the December 7, 1941 extra edition newspaper image announcing the beginning of World War II.

Without the perseverance of my daughter, Stephanie Pope, this episode in my life would have never been written. She persisted for eight years, even to the extent of sending me a sturdy notebook and pen. She won. I consulted with her from time to time and she used her editing skills to put my scribbling in final book form.

I would like to thank my daughter, Ricketta Van Dress, for using her artistic talent to supply the artwork used in this book.

I would also like to thank my granddaughter, Ann Marie Van Dress, for her care in the copy edit of my war memoir.

Lastly, I want to thank my family, one and all for their support.

R J Van Dress
April, 2015

PROLOGUE

The last barrier to the invasion of Japan fell with a mighty crash in the eighty-one days of battle on the bastion of Okinawa... It was seventy days later when the war ended in the Pacific... There were neither sufficient men nor adequate bases close enough to Japan to warrant immediate invasion of the home islands, but resources were sufficient with which to attack the outlying precincts.

Most tempting of all were the Ryukyu Islands, incorporated by Tokyo as an integral part of Japan itself....

Below that is the Okinawa group, the largest and most important of all. Every consideration made possession of Okinawa essential. It dominated the entire Ryukyu Archipelago, which served as a bastion protecting the East China and the Yellow Seas. Okinawa in Allied hands would open up the China coast from Foochow to Korea; bring all southern Japan within striking distance of planes; leave Formosa virtually helpless against air and sea attack, and the strangling blockade of the home islands would be drawn even more tightly....

The Okinawa group consists of the main island of Okinawa and fifty-four others of various sizes. Okinawa, some sixty-seven miles long and from three to ten wide, offered many landing beaches, thus giving to the Allies a measure of surprise that was lacking at Iwo....

The island had been heavily fortified, with thousands of caves and man-made strong points invading even the hitherto sacred precincts of

Japanese cemeteries. The enemy developed a series of fine airfields, the principal ones being Naha, Yontan, Yonabaru, and a strip on the island of Ie to the north.

The decision was definitely made—the next and last stepping-stone was Okinawa.

~Francis Trevelyan Miller
"The Battle of Okinawa, April – June 1945: "War at its Worst"

INTRODUCTION

We can say that the soldier is a metaphor, which contains three fundamental features of the human being when he or her is seized by Truth. First, it is an example for everybody, it is a universal address; second, it is an example of what can be done by somebody, when it is thought that nothing is possible; it is the creation of a new possibility; third, it is an example of what is immortal, or eternal, in an action which is devoted to a true Idea. It is the creation of an immanent immortality.

~Alain Badiou, *The Contemporary Figure of the Soldier in Politics and Poetry*, UCLA, 2007

Preceding this introduction is an excerpt from "The Battle For Okinawa". The excerpt appears as the prologue in this memoir and contains Francis Trevelyan Miller's historical description.[1] This description is a lead-in for what guided me to recognize the need for getting the story this memoir contains into print.

I discover Miller's historical account on-line, which is why I give the on-line reference in the footnote. One will find this description in its entirety in Chapter 102 of the book, *History of World War II* (Philadelphia: Universal Book & Bible House, 1945.) It is published as an "Armed Services Memorial Edition" for our returning WWII servicemen.

Miller's book provides "an official" or "historical" account

---

1 See Prologue p. iii

of the war. One will find an accounting of, as Miller's book unfolds it, the movement of the 7th Division in 1945 between June 4th and June 21st, as well as the moment General Buchner loses his life. My father's memoir vividly recalls the few precious hours prior to General Buckner's death. My father has asked that Miller's account of General Buckner's death be included as a historical supplement to his memoir. You will find this account toward the end of this book in the unpublished leather-bound addition.

I move between my father's narrative and official accounts to compose this introduction, as well as a few other perspectives gathered in my lengthy survey of literary and historical material about the war years. I will turn back later in this introduction to share with you a perspective on the image of the Japanese soldier as a "suicide" "Jap"; turning it in a poetic way to open space for rethinking on what, to me, is quite an unsettling image. Before I turn back in this direction, I want to first provide you a primary assertion and secondly, peel back and render visible some of the literary socio-political layers surrounding the image of the metaphorical "soldier" and "hero" the way our historical and literary collective imagination contains it.

Narratives and Points of View

The official historical account, which appears in the prologue to this memoir, fails to mention the battle to take hill 153 and this may or may not be by historical design. However, my point in mentioning it is the following; the "official" account is not told from the *point of view of the soldier in the foxhole* as is this narrative recounted in my father's war memoir. I suggest one should turn to memoirs like the one my father has written as a way of retrieving soulfully lived things - sidelined or relegated to the margins by "official" renderings; for these things may become silenced and never told otherwise.

The historical importance of memoir writing is one truth I learn as a result of working with my father in the writing of his war memoir. In my research I uncover the image of the soldier as a poetic figure in the spirit of the times, just as the thought occurs to me to hold the official account suspect. The soldier as a metaphorical poet is an abstraction for what is lacking. I have a hunch, in other words, that the so-called reality of the official account "ain't exactly real". [2] As a result of this hunch my research leads me to trace the image of the archetypal soldier through the poetry and prose of Wallace Stevens. I will return to this thought shortly.

Depersonalizing The Personal

Immanently so, as I take in the printed page and work with the spirit of the story getting the story into manuscript form, I begin to have the feeling the poetic layer in a personal narrative depersonalizes story; my encounter with the soldier image in the story is not my father in the sense of the father I know literally as "father". The soldier is the youth who went to war that I never knew. The personal story now told moves the story to another register of awareness, depersonalizing the image of the soldier in the story. The literal is relaxing its grip over the image literally in writing it down, and the final lines of the memoir are suddenly truer for it. A man is in the making all along where there is no man before say the closing lines of my father's memoir.

On a deeper level the memoir stories the death of the soldier in the death of his youth. Thinking this and writing it now causes me to remember my father saying to me the day he reads me his memoir out loud how when he comes home from war he feels like an old man. In

---

2 Also, this "hunch" of mine..." is comin' from another kind of feel/that ain't exactly real/ or real but ain't exactly "there"..." ~Leonard Cohen, "Democracy Is Coming To The USA" © 1992 Sony/ATV Songs LLC, Stranger Music Inc. Cohen begins writing the lyrics to this song in 1988; more than 30 verses are discarded but retrieved as part of the heritage of spoken word poetry. Of this poetic experience Cohen writes, "...occasioned by the collapse of the Berlin Wall, it is a song where there's no inside and no outside. This is just the life of the democracy. It isn't imposed from above. It isn't connected to a Democratic victory or a Republican victory. It's coming through a hole in the wall, it's coming through a crack; it's coming imperial, mysterious in amorous array. It is the religion of the West. It's just starting....It is part of the appetite for fraternity and for equality that we have that has been animated in our hearts by the whole experiment. But we're just at the beginning; we're just at the edge of it. "Diamonds In The Lines", http://www.leonardcohen-prologues.com/democracy.htm accessed 1-28-14.

fact, he says to me, he feels older than his mother!

Storied this way the soldier metaphor crosses enemy lines, racial and religious points of view, and gender and generational divides. Somehow the point of view from the soldier in the foxhole renders a story more humanly told. Such moments engulf us where soul eats death, as if death itself dies and a spirit, not of the times but of our depths enflames within what thereafter remains to us immortally alive—this is something more real because it's been lived within, recognized consciously, and rendered conscious in language. There is no outside this context. The soldier, as subjectivity in the making (en poieses) of the man, has no outer-life except for the way his inner image of the soldier becomes embodied in the language of a story that lives in us all.

My first assertion is a way of pointing out the historical value to posterity of this personal account. On one hand is the way it fills in what official accounts leave uncounted; the "thousand faces" of the myth of the hero, as Joseph Campbell pictures it, as opposed to "the one face" of "a thousand heroes", such as intends the "veiled" account in Francis Trevelyan Miller's "official" version of the Battle for Okinawa. What is intended *for* returning servicemen is in service *to* a mythology *of* some politic and/or politics; but, if we only notice such little things we discover our prepositions present us with propositions—more than one. A mouth piece of the one face of things as they are staged "officially" is a kind of muzzle over the many mouths of things speaking new potentials as they are rendering themselves over and over in the mimesis of our life experience.

One may imagine the fillings of memoir writing are filling indeed; such are memories told, each from a point of view as one of many mouths in many days living things that satisfy us deeply in the seat of the soul where inner and outer meet (Novalis). This is where personal narration turns over what is literally and factually lived to resurrect from within a more poignant (ab) stracted truth in the form of our collective soldier-as-image—the image standing in for the coming-to-consciousness of a formerly unknown psychic content. To tell one's own story of battle is an activity of psychological man. Psychological man is the inner man in contact with himself; we feel him present. Beyond this man lies another, the mythopoetic man. Mythopoetic man goes further in the telling of the story. He helps what is outside the story (in us) step into the pages of the book and allows the reader to see the world from the immanence of the soldier's foxhole, the way it was, the way he knows it still.

"Soldier" As Metaphor

The soldier is American culture's *poetic figure* seized by what Adiou calls "Truth". Yet, who may presuppose to know to what this refers let alone may mean! By the end of this memoir, and to my father recounting his story of going to war and looking back, "Truth" carries a "real" imprint, one he sums up thusly, "I leave home at nineteen a boy; I return a man."

Curious about this "death" of the boy in the imagination of the memoir's central literary *mythologem* [3], boy/soldier/man, I seek out the image of the soldier in the prose and poetry of the contemporary, American poet of my father's youth, Wallace Stevens. Why Stevens? Mr. Stevens is a young man during WWI and an elder man during the 1940's when my father is a young man preparing to enter battle. Stevens begins publishing most of his poetry and prose during the '40's. A number of his poems have as their central focus the soldier metaphor. Stevens wrestles with the catastrophic inability of language to apprehend let alone represent wartime suffering. How shall the soldier as poet re-presence through the weight of grievances in past disasters? How shall he himself be able to recognize and grasp it with no words for it going before it or afterward? Stevens' poetics is a fascinating trace in close scrutiny of such questions. Let me present one of Stevens' thoughts as I speak to my father's writing style.

Hero Language in Wartime

My father's war memoir is written in a very factual way.

---

3 Basic and/or recurrent theme of myth

There is a minimalism in expression going on and a worded sparseness in details and descriptions prevails. One could call this a *realistic grammar*. [4] Part of this writing style has to do with how writing is taught to young high school students in my father's day; but, from another side, from within, there is a consideration taking hold of a dialectical exchange incited between imagination and the consciously real. I would be remiss if I didn't point this out. As a poet of the times, Stevens becomes concerned with this wartime depth struggle going on in the American psyche and writes a small prose passage amplifying his thought about it just after the publishing of "Examination Of The Hero In A Time Of War," the final poem in the book, *Parts Of A World* (1942). Stevens notes, "In the presence of the violent reality of war, consciousness takes the place of imagination. Consciousness of an immense war is consciousness of fact." [5] When Stevens uses the word, "hero" he means "soldier". [6] The soldier is fully conscious in coming home from war of the immensity of what war, in fact, "is". Seeing this, I'm further incensed by attempts to give returning servicemen sterile versions of so profound a thing they've lived as soldiers.

Wallace Stevens goes on to indicate the poetry of any work of the imagination always undertakes this ongoing struggle with wartime's matter of fact; poetic language and poetic imagery is basic to it, even illustrates it; this inner struggle continues onward during times of peace. Stevens thinks the soldier is poet before which all metaphors for death collapse in the presence of what the world of the soldier embodies that cannot be told. Before a word is spoken, the soldier-as-poet has read his world as a poetic text and what the metaphorical soldier-as-poet of the text itself expresses in its soul-writ—sparse as it may be, goes beyond philosophy.

Stevens is also concerned with the manly image that is the

---

4 "A shift from a peacetime to a wartime economy…results in a shift from an idealistic to a realistic grammar." Kenneth Burke, "War and Cultural Life" in James Longenbach, *Wallace Stevens: The Plain Sense of Things*, "Rethinking War" p. 202.
5 See Lee M Jenkins, *Wallace Stevens: Rage For Order* footnote 16, p. 152.
6 Ibid.

man-in-the-making, both the one that goes to war during wartime, and the one who does not; both the son of the mother who goes to war, and the son in the mother who does not. How a mother and son, in matters of fact, share the intimacies of such space looms here. "Femininity" is the cultural term that most references this wordless space to Stevens. Literary history and feminism both indicate this space is the maiden well of the unsaid where coalesce poetic matters of fact. Stevens who is like the son in the mother and the mother herself, is absent from the foxhole and battle field. Stevens, like mothers of soldiers, does not go to war but as poet enters a foxhole of another sort terribly concerned as he is about making as strong a contribution as possible toward deepening the cultural psyche's awareness in such catastrophic, poetic matters of fact as is wartime.

My father is the youngest of four sons and two daughters born to his mother and father, my Grandma and Grandpa Van Dress. All four sons serve simultaneously in the Armed Services during WWII. In a letter to my grandparents The State Department acknowledges this tremendous sacrifice to the nation on the part of their family. A photo of the letter is included in this memoir. Each of my grandma's sons comes home from the war and each return lightens her heart considerably; but, during the war years she may have carried in her heart the greatest angst for the well-being of my father since his role in the war took him to the front lines.

My father's family is of Italian descent. His mother, father, sisters, and brothers are dark-haired and dark-eyed. Somewhere in the family gene pool, however, there is blue-eyed kin because my father has blue eyes. My father is grandma's "blue-eyed son." Perhaps it is the poet in me in touch with the poet-as-soldier in the story-in-the-making going on in the man-in-the-making written down in my father or perhaps it is the old folk saying about eyes being portals to what presence shows itself even though it's not exactly "there"; or perhaps it is the image of the blue-eyed son that is really marking for me the poetic space that most concerns the poet, Stevens. Something makes metaphorical the motif of "the blue-eyed son". It is an image doubling for the memoir itself, the entirety of it, the enormity of it—particularly what, in parts, cannot be told. "The blue-eyed son" for me becomes a space where the disparate sides of sons and mothers in son and mother return to each other and remain with each other and belong together in poetic matter of fact. This notion sits well with me again when my father later tells me he will title his WWII memoir, *Dear Mom*.

Mother and Son

Where have you been my blue-eyed son?
Where have you been my darling young one?

~Bob Dylan, "A Hard Rain's A-Gonna Fall"

There are poetic matters of fact that are wartime experiences so catastrophic that one must feel into them because they are not nameable. When you first encounter the soldier in his foxhole it will be raining hard. Remember this poetic space and that conveyance of immediacy that goes unspoken here. Imbedded here is the underground of the soldier's endearments, the misery of his burdens, which he cannot shed and which cannot be said.

There is a letter my father writes to his mother explaining to her how he decides to take a job as company clerk because he realizes it will relieve her anxieties for him fighting at the front. There is another letter that he writes to his mother which tells her how her letters to him got him through so many days. We don't have her letters now but we are lucky to have his letters to her.

When my father comes home from war and finally greets his mother again, the memoir tells us they embrace each other for a long time. There are many moments like this where endearment and burden, reunion and separation, and joy and sacrifice surface and wordlessly sense what gives body to the soldier-as-metaphor who is returning it to us. Let me further suggest that it is this heroic language which gives to us that rare poetic glimpse in *sudden salience* [7] of an otherwise invisibly embodied belonging together.

A Spirit of Times; A Spirit of Depths

In matters of fact a spirit of times is one kind of real; a spirit of depths, another. The spirit of the depths, speaking in the man telling the story of the boy as a soldier in the presence of heroic things, speaks the poetic language of the soldier in the foxhole through a *voice from "down under."* You will see this phrase used in the memoir. When you do, link it back to this spot in my introduction and sit with it awhile because this is the depth soul home-making; by and by it reveals to us in our meditation and in our dreams, reflections, and memories that which is meaningful in what we face (that is at bottom most precious after all).

In terms of this distinction between inner and outer things, between the spirit of times and the spirit of the inwardly real, are the writings of Carl Jung. Jung begins to understand the hero archetype functions as a purveyor of cultural mythology. He writes:

But whom do people kill? They kill the noble, the brave, the heroes. They take aim at these and do not know that with these they mean themselves. They should sacrifice the hero in themselves and because they don't know this, they kill their courageous brother.[8]

The Suicide Japs

According to the historical voice we collectively inherit, one documented in footnote 22 of this memoir (see p.43), for the Japanese, "surrender deviates from the demands of samurai code of

---

7 "We can occupy a day, a routine day, unaware of the mechanisms upon which we rely for a sense of belonging, of comfort, of connection with our territory – territory in all sorts of senses: geographic, civic, temporal, social, emotional." *A Sudden Salience: Narrative, Poetry And Architecture, Pt.2 Dissertation,* 2010, Kate Coghlan, Edinburg College of Art, Edinburg, UK, The RIBA Presidents Student Medals Awards, http://www.presidentsmedals.com/Entry-12620 accessed 3-31-15.

8 p. 28 The Red Book.

conduct." It is important to remember this is a poetic image of the soldier, *aka the soldier as hero*. It insists a Japanese soldier does not surrender. He commits hara-kiri.

There is a little incident that occurs in which the story of hara-kiri unfolds differently on the battlefield in Okinawa just before the taking of hill 153. Just as my father tells it, from the point of view of the soldier as he is fighting on the front lines while deep within "the heart of Jap territory," something unexpected happens. That phrase, "the heart of Jap territory" is taken directly from the memoir (p41). My father writes:

We now expect a banzai charge. I can hear the Japs talking. They are high on saké and yelling "Banzai". Since we are very close, we prepare by fixing bayonets to our M-1 rifles. One Japanese yells "Banzai!" I see him rush out over a big boulder. But, just as fast he runs back to safety. It is really very intense as we expect a terrible bayonet slaughter. But, even so, it is rather comical the way it never happens.

In the story that unfolds one can see a change taking place deep in the collective heart as it individually speaks through the Japanese soldier fighting on the front lines—for the Japanese soldier employs his courage in another kind of very courageous way. He slays the hero within himself and is going beyond the spirit of times to that of the heart just as Jung suggests one need do. In this moment, in an aesthetic, poetic way, the Japanese soldiers' body movement in the little story my father tells is signaling a kind of *hermetic* movement at work within poetic images themselves, such an image as is the soldier as poet.

The word 'hermetic' is connected to Greek imagination in stories of the god, Hermes, and again through Jung, to seemingly mysterious, little understood, and hidden psychological transformations underway. Greek stories of Hermes often carry their own kind of humor and Hermes is very much a divine figure present on battlefields. When Hermes shows up one can expect the unexpected. As myth stories it, Hermes carries *deadly* "hero" soul away from the battlefield when he carries away the souls of dead heroes to their places of rest in the Elysian Fields. In this hermetic, archetypal sense, the Japanese soldiers' heroic gesture is reclaiming for the soul of the world a spirit of depths in an individuating nobility, bravery, and manhood which transcend the physical battlefield. I once think it is the dropping of the two atomic bombs to be what saves and brings my father home from war; but now, I am no longer quite certain. One may argue the dropping of the two atomic bombs are the physical cause leading to Dad's homecoming; but I sense the secret cause for his physical return is carried by the hermetic soul contained in this story.

In Closing

From literary and psychological perspectives one may reason that whatever is marginalized in official accounts may be returned and indeed does return from confinement in our depths embedded in memories, dreams, and reflections as we tell our stories. Such things as these gather into distinct, heart-felt thoughts and are taken center-stage particularly in memoir writing. The depth imprint left upon the brow of our soul's logical life thickens our connections to each other and marks the edges in us in specific ways just as it informs our personal experience. In sharing such stories as written narratives, where once we thought we suffered alone, we are now with a whole world lost in our experiences.

There is a moment when my father pauses from reading his memoir out loud to me. He says, "You finish reading it to me." I do. A silence falls between us for a while. Then he says to me he doesn't understand why even after so many years have passed he cannot read the story all the way through without weeping. It bears repeating. A whole world is with us always lost in our experiences; lost in our experiences, what makes us weep. In sharing such stories as narratives, what makes us weep is found again. No matter how sparse the language, the feeling is found in our writing and we feel it too… the world weeping with us.

Our deep truths are the ones most worth handing from generation to generations ever after. They fill our best stories and become the stories most worth telling. No matter how minimalist the writing style, catastrophic things in matters of fact convey themselves.

It is my hope the closing of my introduction to my father's memoir remains enjambed and that it opens a space for you to interrogate the soldier in the foxhole you meet here. Take over now. You finish reading it to me.

––––––––––––––––––––––––––––––

Works Cited

Coghlan, Kate. A Sudden Salience: Narrative, Poetry And Architecture, Pt.2 Dissertation, 2010. Edinburg College of Art, Edinburg, UK, The RIBA Presidents Student Medals Awards, http://www.presidentsmedals. com/Entry-12620 accessed 3-31-15.

Cohen, Leonard. "Democracy Is Coming to the USA". ©1992 Sony/ ATV Songs LLC, Stranger Music Inc.

_____. "Diamonds In The Lines". Interview http://www. leonardcohen-prologues.com/democracy.htm accessed 1-28-14.

Dylan, Bob. A Hard Rain's A-Gonna Fall. ©1963 Warner Bros. Inc. renewed 1991 by Special Rider Music. Song lyrics, bobdylan.com / http://www.bobdylan.com/us/songs/hard-rains-gonna-fall accessed 1-29-14.

Higa, Takejiro. American Intelligence Service. The Hawaii Nisei Story: Americans of Japanese Ancestry During WWII, "The Battle of Okinawa". Ted Tsukijama. http://nisei.hawaii.edu/object/ io_11493161855200.html accessed 1-29-14.

Jenkins, Lee M.. Wallace Stevens: Rage For Order. Portland: Suxxex Academic Press, 2000.

Jung, Carl. The Red Book Sonu Shamdasani, Editor. Norton: New York, 2009 First Edition.

Longenbach, James. Wallace Stevens: The Plain Sense of Things. New York: Oxford Press, 1991.

Miller, Francis Trevelyan. "The Battle of Okinawa, April – June 1945: "War at its Worst", Salt of America.com, article number 204. Date article uploaded 01-29-2013. http://saltofamerica.com/contents/displayArticle.aspx?18_204 accessed October 21, 2013.

I.

Foreword

I am a sixteen year old high school sophomore at St John High School (now Central Catholic High School) in Canton, Ohio when, on December 7, 1941, I hear a newsboy yelling,

"Extra! Extra! Read all about it!"

I wonder what this is all about, I am thinking. Later that day I read that…

"*The United States of America has been suddenly and deliberately attacked by naval and Air Forces of the Empire of Japan. Our President, Franklin D. Roosevelt asks that Congress declare that since the unprovoked and dastardly attack by Japan a state of war exists between the United States and the Japanese Empire.*

Little do I realize that some three years later I will be in a combat infantry machine gun squad in what is now known as one of the bloodiest battles of the Pacific and the last battle of World War II, *The Battle of Okinawa.*

Today my grandchildren want to know about this time in my life. They ask

"Grandpa, what happened to you? What did you do?"

Well, here is my story.

II.

1941-1944

I am both a sophomore in high school and a newsboy with a Canton Repository newspaper route consisting of approximately eighty customers. I make $7.50 per week. The economy is booming. Many more jobs are becoming available and, although I go out for football in my freshman year, in my sophomore year I decide to get another job and earn more money.

fig 2-a **Ron standing in front of the Sterling Bakery truck he drove in the 1940's**

School is out and I am walking across the play-ground when I suddenly hear the voice of Coach Del Hal-prin calling out to me as he hurries to catch up with me. He wants to know why I am not going out for football. I say:

"I want to get a job and earn some money."

"You will be working all your life; you should reconsider," Coach responds.

I choose to work. All

through high school I work various jobs. I am an usher at the Strand Theatre, a stock boy at Sterling Bakery *(fig. 2-a)* and an employee of both Winbigler's Sunoco service and Westlawn Cemetery. Coach Halprin was right.

Working while going to high school affects my grades. In fact, as Monsignor Graham distributes the report cards, he quips, *"You're going to drown in all those C's!"* Although I am not a good student, I do excel in speech. Father Holbrook selects me to star in a play called "Dust of the Road" where I play the part of Judas Iscariot. The play earns a welcome monetary reward for the school. That same year I win first prize of twenty-five dollars reciting The Gettysburg Address in a competition sponsored by the American Legion. And so, as WWII begins, it is this way for me until my senior year in 1943.

In the month of October I am startled to receive from Stark County Local Board #5 an order dated October 8th telling me to report for induction *(fig. 2b)*. You see, I am not yet a graduate of high school. My mother and I immediately appeal to the board and I receive a deferment for the time being. We both breathe a sigh of relief until the following July.

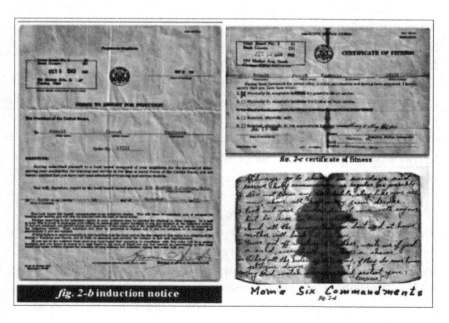

fig. 2-c certificate of fitness

fig. 2-b induction notice

Mom's Six Commandments

On July 14, 1944 I receive a physical examination *(fig. 2-c)* and am found physically fit and acceptable for general military service such that on September 15, 1944, at the age of nineteen, I am officially inducted into The Army of the United States of America.

Mom's Six Commandments

Before I leave for basic training my dear mother gives to me six commandments that she wishes me to follow *(fig. 2-d)*. Written down for me in her neat handwriting, I have it still.

You may be curious about Ron's mom's six commandments. Here is a close up of the note she gave him before leaving for basic training.

I am sent to Cleveland where I spend one day, then on to Camp Atterbury, Indiana for two weeks. I receive indoctrination into the army. In my opinion I am being "brain washed" into the army. I am told there are three ways to do things, the right way, the wrong way and the army way and from then on I am to do things the army way. I contemplate this statement briefly trying to make sense of it and finally just accept it. While at Camp Atterbury I experience an awful feeling of home sickness. I cannot eat. I cannot sleep. I want to lie down but I cannot do that. This lasts about 48 hours before it leaves me; I never experience homesickness again.

I am now informed I will go to Camp Blanding, Florida for seventeen weeks of combat infantry basic training. Before leaving for Camp Blanding I am administered many different inoculations and receive a physical examination from head to toe. I learn my blood type is "A". Throughout my army career I receive the following vaccinations, many administered periodically: small pox, influenza, triple typhoid, tetanus toxoid, yellow fever, cholera and a bubonic plague shot I will never forget! It may be the medics administer me an overdose because it feels like I have contracted the disease; it keeps me awake all night!

To get to Florida I go by train through the states of Kentucky, Tennessee and Georgia. Travel is one of the more pleasant army necessities. At Camp Blanding we are assigned to barracks alphabetically. Because of this I miss bunking with my two friends, Jim Malloy and Don Wechter. As I recall there are eight men in a barrack; each barrack has one of the eight men designated in charge. I don't remember the name of the man in charge of our barrack. One man is selected to lead the platoon. He happens to bunk in our barrack. He is tall and appears to be the image of a leader. His name is Tomkinson.

While at camp Blanding I am trained to march, shoot and salute. I spend many hours firing types of weaponry: the M-1 rifle, the carbine and the 30 caliber water cooled machine gun. Of the three, the machine gun turns out to be my principle weapon. It is fun to fire the machine gun at night. Every 6th round is a tracer bullet that one can see racing through the night sky.

I am also taught to field strip and clean my weaponry and then how to put them back together again while blindfolded. I also learn how to throw a grenade into a pillbox and how to fire a bazooka. I learn that if the enemy throws a grenade and it lands near where I and fellow soldiers are, I should throw myself on top of it so that my body absorbs the impact of the explosion protecting my comrades. What I think of that idea I'll leave to the imagination of the reader.

As you may well see by now, the end result of my basic training is to become a tough, cagy, and alert soldier. After this training I must be able to function as a member of a combat team. During basic I am constantly reminded that if I fail to do it right when I go "down under", my chances of going back home are slim. Going "down under" is army slang for going into combat. Of all the various kinds of combat training I guess I mind bayonet practice more than anything else. In this practice we are required to affix our bayonet to the end of our M-1 rifle and plunge it into a sack while yelling "deep plunge" and

23

"withdraw" and we are to continue doing this until given a command to stop.

I shall say here that basic training is not all work and no play. I do get to go on pass to St. Augustine and Gainesville with my two closest friends Don Wechter and Jim Malloy. St. Augustine is a historical city with many sites to see. The picture of Jim, Don, and I on a lion is typical of the many statues at St Augustine. (see insert fig. 2-e) Gainesville is small and quiet, a residential community. I am also able to get a special pass when I receive a surprise visit from my cousin, Ellen Collete and her husband who

fig. 2-f
Don & Ron with the Atlantic Ocean in the background

fig. 2-e
from left to right Ron, Don & Jim

fig. 2-g
Jim & Ron / (Same ocean!)

is an army cook with the rank of Tech Sgt.. Because of his rank I am able to get the special pass. The other photos of us show the Atlantic Ocean in the background. (fig. 2-f and 2-g)

There are some intense moments in basic training. I remember one incident where a recruit pulls the pin from a grenade releases the handle making it "live" and then freezes in fear of a live grenade in his hand. The Sargent-In-Charge has to rush in, grab the grenade from the recruit and hurl it into the pill box before it explodes.

There are also some comical incidents, too. For example, while firing on the rifle range, some recruits miss the target entirely causing

Maggie's drawers[1] to go up. We laugh at this but later pay for laughing because we have to take our day off on Sunday to set targets for those who "bolo".[2] Training culminated with two weeks spent on bivouac, but because of the urgent need for combat replacements my bivouac is shortened. Bivouac means sleeping on the ground in a pup tent. All activities are performed without shelter. December nights and early mornings are damp and cold in stark Florida. I think I should relate here that there are two disappointing incidents during basic training. One occurs the evening before I set out on bivouac.

After the evening meal it is my custom to go to the PX (Post Exchange). Upon my return I discover one of my two wool blankets are missing. Since all members of the barracks are present I say, "*Who took my blanket; one of them is missing?*" No one responds. I then say, "*I'm going away for fifteen minutes. When I come back, if the missing blanket is not back on my bed, I'm going to report it to the cadre.*" My actions follow my words. And, when I return, the missing blanket is back on my bed. I direct my next question to the man in charge of the barracks. "*What's going on?*" At this point Tomkinson says belligerently, "*I took it.*" I could not hide my disappointment. I let loose with a lecture. The man-in-charge knows he did not do his job and the culprit hangs his head in shame. After three months in basic training together one should be able to trust the man next to him!

The other disappointment I encounter occurs in the early course of my training. Our company is required to take physical and mental tests to select men qualified to drive military vehicles. Because few drivers are needed the tests are extremely difficult to eliminate all but the most qualified. Only three men pass the test and I am one

---

1 Maggie's drawers refer to a red disc used on the rifle range to signify missing the target as in "he fires a clip but all he gets Maggie's drawers."
2 Bolo is Army or soldier slang for missing the target, one of several meanings for the term. See also footnote five. In the U.S. military the slang term, "to bolo" —to fail a test, exam or evaluation, originates from the Philippine-American guerilla forces during World War II; those guerillas who failed to demonstrate proficiency in marksmanship were issued bolos instead of firearms so as not to waste scarce ammunition. (see Wikipedia, http://webcache.googleuser-content.com/search?q=cache:kLz75x8KeHsJ:en.wikipedia.org/wiki/Bolo_knife+&cd=1&hl=en&ct=clnk&gl=us accessed August 21, 2013.) Among recruits, bolo is a kind of jab at another recruit's poor marksmanship.

of the three. When I return to the barracks, I inform the Sargent-in-charge that I am to report to obtain my military drivers permit. He unhesitatingly and brusquely refuses my request. Needless to say I am disappointed. However, his refusal may have saved my life. Later on in my story you will see why I say this.

* * *

III.

No Longer A Recruit

Upon completion of Basic Training we are no longer recruits. We are now soldiers. I weigh 125 pounds when I begin training and 155 pounds these fifteen weeks later. (*fig. 3-a and 3-b*) My training is reduced from seventeen weeks to fifteen weeks due to the urgent need for combat infantry soldiers. I never receive a furlough during my whole time (more than two years!) in the Army, the bulk of which is spent overseas. I complete Basic in December. Like the song goes, I write my mother to tell her, "I'll be home for Christmas." And, I am! (*fig. 3-c*)

fig. 3-a Ron, age 19 barracks, Camp Blanding, FL.

fig. 3-c Mom & Ron Christmas Day, Monday December 25, 1944

fig. 3-b Ron in December, 1944 Camp Blanding, FL.

"A five-day delay en route"

Since all good things must come to an end, on Tuesday December 26th, with a fist full of tickets that will take me from my home at 516 Lincoln Avenue N.W. in Canton, Ohio to the West Coast and specifically, to San Francisco, California, I say good-bye and am off. I feel a bit anxious, but Duty calls.

My first stop is Chicago, Illinois. I am able to attend a stage show where the original members of The Ink Spots are performing. My train then moves on to Iowa and Omaha, Nebraska where I must change trains, off again to Salt Lake City, Utah. The train rides over the Great Salt Lake and continues on to Reno, Nevada and finally San Francisco. I'm not sure how long it takes to travel from Ohio to California by train. It may have taken anywhere from three to five days of eating and sleeping on the train. I bunk at Fort Ord for two weeks and am able to go on pass to Salinas and Monterey. I think I am going to leave for overseas but instead go on to Fort Lawton, Washington where I spend one month.

At each stop we soldiers perform time on various training duties. I notice the air in Washington is different from most other places I visit. It is very invigorating. In all my stateside duty I am never as free as when I am here at Fort Lawton even though, while there, I do the hardest K.P. [3] of my Army career. I think I can say that Seattle is my favorite army city. I attend an ice skating show. While at the rink I telephone Mom as I know I am heading for overseas and "the Lord knows what." I speak to Mom and brother, Troy, who happens to be home on furlough. It is the last time I speak to anyone from the family until I come home for good.

* * *

---

3 Army acronym for kitchen police.

IV.

Overseas, 1945

fig. 4-a a typical scene of some of the 3,000 troops aboard
ship on the Pacific Ocean, headed for Hawaii, 1945.

fig. 4-b Ron with the hula dancer
Honolulu, Hawaii, 1945

I think I am going to leave for overseas from Seattle Harbor. Instead I travel to Portland, Oregon where I finally board the ship that will sail to Hawaii. There are three thousand troops aboard. Suddenly I realize the military in charge is confusing the enemy by not leaving from California or Washington. It is a five day voyage over the ocean and, although I enjoy the first part of the trip, nearly everyone is seasick. (fig. 4-a)

While nearing the island the first thing I see looks like a pineapple lying in the ocean. As we sail nearer the pineapple is getting larger and begins rising out of the ocean. By the time we finally dock I see how the pineapple is on a very tall tower on the land.[4] Pineapple

---

4 The pineapple replica most likely is marking a pineapple processing cannery on the island. Chances are what is being described is the Dole Water Tower Pineapple which, in 1945, sits atop Dole Cannery, Iwilei. The "pineapple" can be seen as one enters Honolulu Harbor.

fields are nearby. We dock in Honolulu and are taken to our barracks in trucks.

While in Hawaii on the island of Oahu we continue military training. For about two weeks I undergo what is called "jungle training". While walking through an area that simulates a jungle atmosphere, targets spring up from either the ground and/or on trees and, in a moment's notice, I have to decide if I am seeing a soldier from my own armed forces or one from the enemy's forces. Should I fire upon my own side, I will have *"bolo'd".*[5]

I go on pass to Honolulu with my friend, Wetzel. He has a Hawaiian hula girl tattooed on his arm. I cannot find anything that suits me so I forego getting a tattoo. I sure am glad and for more than one reason! Wetzel suffers for a few days until his arm heals. To compensate for not getting a tattoo I decide to get my picture taken with a Hawaiian hula dancer, grass skirt and all. (*see fig. 4-b*)

fig. 4-a The Ship's Wake

fig. 4-c Ron on deck looking at the ship's wake.

After a couple of months we are on the move again. We board ship headed this time for the island of Saipan in the Marshalls. We stop off one night for refueling at Eniwetok [6] but are not permitted to get off the ship. My recollection of the island is just a strip of land in the ocean.

5 Bolo is military slang having various meanings. 1. One meaning is "Be On the Look Out." A bolo is usually a list with descriptions of vehicles or personnel to be on the lookout for. 2. Bolo is also slang for no good. Bolo can be used as a noun when something goes wrong as in the following phrase: "That's a bolo." Or it can be used as a verb as in "I bolo'd that task." See http://www.itstactical.com/intellicom/language/military-acronymsterminology-and-slang-reference/ ; see also footnote two.

Saipan, 1945

It takes twenty-two days to reach Saipan. We cannot take a direct route because the waters are mined and there are probably other military reasons as well. When a mine is spotted, the ship's gunner fires at it and blows it up. At one point while we are going through a heavily mined area at night, we are required to line up on deck after dark with life belts prepared to jump overboard, if necessary. As I recall it now, I do not feel apprehensive and am prepared to do just that, if necessary. Fortunately, we make it through the mine field without mishap and are permitted to return to our hammocks. Whereas we can watch movies on deck after dark while going to Hawaii, we cannot do this while going to Saipan. We are in more hazardous waters and nearer the enemy. Smokers cannot smoke after dark and lights are prohibited. *(See fig. 4-c and fig. 4-d)*

We arrive at Saipan and are informed that "Japs"[7] are still on the island. We bunk on the ground which is mostly coral rock. We shelter in pup tents[8] the first week—not very comfortable! We observe that a shower room is just completed but goes unused so Wetzel, Vargo and I decide to move in. It is just like having a private room. I receive orders for duty personnel where I run a mimeograph machine.[9]

One warm day on Saipan I hear the army receives a limited shipment of cold beer and is passing it out. At first I think it is a joke. In my entire army career, the Army never gives out free beer. It is April

---

6 A battle is fought on Eniwetok June, 1944. See D-Day In The Pacific: The Battle of Saipan by Harold J. Goldberg (Indiana: Indiana U Press, 2007) "...Saipan had everything: caves like Tulagi; mountains and ridges like the 'Canal'; a reef nearly as treacherous as Betio's; a swamp like Buna; a city to be conquered, like those on Sicily; and death-minded Japs like the defenders of Attu. A lot, for so small an island." With such a description as this landscape in what precedes his arrival in Saipan, it is not so difficult to imagine where this soldier will make his Saipan bunk and lay his head that first week. Not very comfortable, indeed! For his description see the next paragraph.

12, 1945. As I am running toward the beer line word comes over the loud speaker that President Franklin D. Roosevelt has died. I pause momentarily from what I am doing to listen; then I continue on. We will now have a new Commander-in-Chief, President Harry S. Truman. I hear no comments from my fellow soldiers.

Because of the prolific mosquito population on Saipan we are required to take Atabrine tablets; I believe these are a substitute for quinine. Continued use of Atabrine will give your skin a yellowish tint. When I find out the tablets do not prevent malaria, I avoid taking the pill altogether.

After several weeks on Saipan we are ordered to assemble. A general comes forth and begins to speak. He is giving us a pep talk, a talk something like a coach gives to his players before the football game begins. The only thing I remember about his talk, one which lasts about thirty minutes, is when he says, "You men will be coming back, you boys won't." I did not like this. I think it is the wrong thing to say. I know then we are going "down under." I am right. We are going to be replacements for the soldiers that are wounded or killed in the Battle of Okinawa. This battle begins April 1, 1945.

* * *

_____

7 The term, "Japs" is Army slang for enemy Japanese soldiers during the WWII era. During wartime, war is waged not only on political, economic, and military fronts but war is also waged on the social or "home" front. Such remnant words in our speech as is the term, "Japs" still leaves its trace or mark or likeness on these times for what an imaginally embodied (as opposed to an imaginary image), collectively held imagination's "citizen body" of the 1940's social sphere of confrontation was once like. In this other space, the imaginal one, a likeness for the "like" through which the slang word imitates still operates now but on a residual, not conscious, non-personal level of collective, objective imagination. Approaching the "ghost" word haunting the 1940's language embodying the national soul and the spirit of those times is a kind of soul retrieval necessary to help in understanding felt-senses. Such retrieval will require a descent into a language usage such as "Japs" to unpack more of the term's dark, collectively held imagination (dark as in hidden and also as in something carrying varied shades of meaning more than just one thing.) For a brief look at the mythopoetic image, "Japs" see the section of my introduction titled "The Suicide Japs".

8 "Pup" tent is a military term for shelter tent. A shelter tent is a small military tent housing two men. It does not have a floor nor does it have windows.

9 A mimeograph is a printing device in which a waxed paper stencil, cut by a typewriter rotates on a drum, ink from which penetrates the cut areas and is deposited on a sheet of paper with each revolution.

V.

Okinawa, 1945

We board a ship headed for Okinawa. With about eight travel days behind us we can now hear shooting and what sound like artillery and mortar shells going off. The ship makes its way to what seems to be no more than a few miles from shore and then stops. We climb over the side of the ship with all our gear; we climb down rope ladders into LST's [10] that are waving and bobbing below. We climb down; but, to what? We do not know. One soldier loses his grip on the ropes he hangs onto and plummets into the LST. Fortunately he is near the bottom and is not injured.

Whereas married men with children are assigned to the artillery, married men without children are assigned to mortar section. Since I am single, I am assigned to the machine gun section of Company "D" 17th Infantry Regiment, Seventh Division. It happens that Company "D" has just been relieved from battle; they are in a rest area when I report for duty.

* * *

---

10 The brain child of Sir Winston Churchill, the tank landing ship or LST is a ship that can transport battle tanks and heavy rolling equipment over the sea to forward battle areas and deliver the load directly to beachhead. Proving more versatile and more rugged than even this, the LST transports during WWII general cargo, locomotives, railroad cars, all types of vehicles, prisoners, casualties and fresh troops to replace those wounded or killed in battle. By way of explanation, the "big" guns of the artillery are miles behind the front lines. The motors are closer and the machine guns are on the frontlines.

LETTERS TO MOM

May 12, 1945

Dearest Mother,

You must be worried about me for not having written to you for such a long time, but as usual it was impossible since I went on another Sea Voyage. It seems as soon as I am accustomed to one place I am moved to another.

Pop, Ralph or Chet probably guessed the particular island I was on in the Mariana's—it was Saipan.

I am now on Okinawa: Pop has probably been reading—reading it in the news. From now on, Pop, you can follow the 7th Division Infantry in the news and know where I am.

I got news of Germany surrendering; it made all the boys happy. I'll bet the people

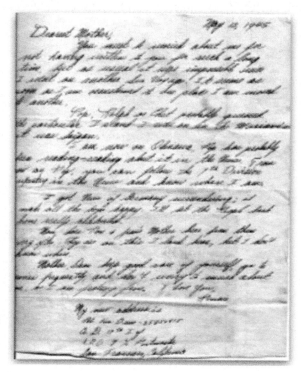

back home really celebrated.

Mom, do Jim and Don's mother hear from them very often? They are on the island here, but I don't know where.

Mother, Dear, keep good care of yourself, go to movies frequently, and don't worry too much about me, as I am fine.

I Love You,
Ronnie

My new address is Pvt. Van Dress -35850415, Co. D. 17th Inf. A.P.O. 7 postmaster, San Francisco, California

* * *

May 15, 1945

Dearest Mother,

How is my sweetheart today? I always say a prayer that she feels well and happy.

In my estimation Okinawa is one of the best islands I've been on so far. The only thing I have found pesty are the fleas and flies. There are sure plenty of burial tombs over here. Maybe you have read something about them in the paper.

Pop, you should see the Okinawan's gardens down here. Cabbage, tomatoes, beans, and corn are plentiful and ripe. But, most of it is going to waste since we placed the Okinawan people in a camp set aside from our troops.

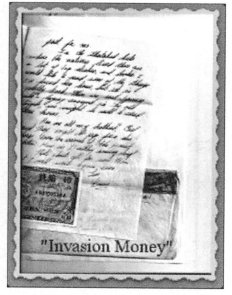

"Invasion Money"

There are a lot of stray horses and goats here. I was trying to catch a horse but it was too fast for me.

In the thatched huts where the natives lived there are a lot of Jap dishes and books. I would like to send some of the things I've found here home, but it is pretty hard. There are real Japanese silks lying around in the old tombs; we might be able to send them home.

How are all my brothers? Carl and Troy might be up for discharge soon on account of the point system. How is Dorothy coming along?

That's about all for now, Mom, but I will write again soon.

Love, Ronnie

P.S. Enclosed is 10 Sen or a "Y.S. Penny". They call it "invasion money."

Active Duty

I pull guard duty every night and go on patrol during the day to insure there are no stray Japs in the area. I play cards with the non-com, the non-commissioned officers and have some fun telling fortunes. One Spanish soldier believes me so much he will not leave me alone. He wants me to tell him more. I feel guilty.

One night I cannot sleep because of terrible pain on my left ear. When I get up next morning and look in a pocket mirror I see a huge lump on my ear which I find out is a carbuncle. I am advised to see our company doctor who is quartered nearby. That is a surprise to me since I do not know we have a doctor! He takes one look at my ear and asks me if I can stand some pain. Before I can answer, he uses his scalpel on my ear. What a relief when all the puss and blood comes out. The pain is gone. Meanwhile, the guys razz me about being wounded before I get into combat. They say I should be awarded the Purple Heart.[11]

I am promoted to PFC (Private First Class) by company order 35 on May 15, 1945.[12] I am lying on my bunk when, after two

---

11 The Purple Heart is awarded to members of the armed forces of the U.S. who are wounded by an instrument of war in the hands of the enemy and posthumously to the next of kin in the name of those who are killed in action or die of wounds received in action. It is specifically a combat decoration. The Purple Heart is established in 1782 and re-established in 1932.

12 Promotion to PFC is done at the company level and announced in company General Orders and the WWII soldier receives a PFC chevron. The designation PFC exists since 1866. From August 5, 1920 to May 28, 1968, the rank insignia for private first class is this single chevron, per War Department Circular No. 303. It doesn't change until 1968 when it becomes a single chevron with one rocker. (see http://en.wikipedia.org/wiki/Private_first_class) PFCs are paid at a slightly higher rate than PVTs (aka "privates".) Each unit is limited in the number of PFC ranks (or ratings) it can have; thusly, the best privates in the unit are supposed to be PFCs and gain the extra few dollars pay.

37

weeks in the rest area (bivouac area) we are informed that we will be "moving up", going into combat. I get kind of a sick feeling to the stomach which passes immediately. After all, this is for what we are trained.[13]

Subsequently the Catholic chaplain invites all the soldiers of the Catholic faith to assemble in a certain area. I remember being surprised at the number of us who assemble. He gives us a brief sermon to prepare us for what we are about to face. It is almost the antithesis of the speech the general gives us on Saipan. The chaplain asks us to make a general confession and gives us absolution followed by Holy Communion. In retrospect I remember thinking how Mom would be pleased to know this but I never tell her because I do not want to worry her unnecessarily.

On Tuesday May 29, 1945 at 14:15 hours[14] we move up to the front in trucks. I am not as excited as I thought I would be. We travel as far in the trucks as is safe, then get off at the Sugar Mill and walk up the valley. We are at the 184th area South of Gava.[15] This is my first night spent in a fox hole.[16] It is not comfortable but I sleep. Our Sgt., "Snake" shares the hole. He is of Mexican descent. They call him Snake because he is good at sneaking up on his prey. I find out just how good later on!

At about this time Mom and Pop receive a letter dated 25 May, 1945. It is from Secretary of War, Henry L. Stimson and it recognizes the fact they have four sons serving in our armed Forces; it recognizes the anguish and anxiety it may be causing them. (See the letter,

---

13 The feeling tone described here is exactly that soul to which the term, "bivouac" refers. Bivouac is a French word containing the image-notion of being on watch or lying in wait. In other words, for two weeks our newly designated PFC has been in bivouac waiting to be called into combat on the front lines of battle.

14 2:15 p.m.

15 Conical Hill

16 A fox hole is a type of defensive fighting position (DFP) adopted in WWII. Sometimes called a "ranger grave", the vertical, bottle-shaped hole allows the soldier to stand and fight with head and shoulders exposed. A fox hole is widened near the bottom to allow the soldier to crouch down while under heavy artillery fire. A fox hole can be enlarged to a two-man fighting position and can contain sumps for water drainage or grenade disposal.

envelope attached.) I do not know if it is sent at this time as a result of my entering combat on Okinawa or if this is just coincidence they receive the letter at this moment in time.

We receive word that one of our planes is dropping fresh bread by parachute. As I look skyward I can see the plane and several parachutes coming down. Three volunteers are needed to go back and retrieve the bread. It needs said here that throughout my Army career I never volunteer for anything. But, since I am a bread lover, particularly after eating dry biscuits in "C" rations,[17] I become one of the volunteers. Three of us head toward the parachutes which are coming down in an open field. What we do not know is that there are snipers hiding in trees left standing or behind rocks and other shelter. They begin firing. We do all we can to get out of there as fast as we can—mostly crawling on our bellies. Thank god we all three made it back, without any bread.

On Wednesday, May 30, 1945 I rise early, eat "C" rations and push off closer to the enemy. It is a four or five mile hike. I am loaded down with my bed roll, all my equipment and two boxes of machine gun ammunition which weighs approximately thirty pounds per box. I am really tired when we reach our destination on a high hill. We set up our machine gun. The entire company is committed to the line south of Yonabaru.[18] A prisoner is captured by 2nd platoon.

We remain here through May 31, 1945, enduring some enemy fire. There are no injuries. June 1, 1945 we move late in the afternoon at the base of the hill. I dig in with Sparks and Mike. We dig the

---

17 "C" rations are canned foods in use during WWII to feed soldiers.
18 See map appendix; for both the map and a courtesy of reuse please see http://commons. wikimedia.org/wiki/File:Okinawa,_April-June_1945-49b_-_Naha-Shuri-Yonabaru.png . Since dad is in the 7th Division he pushes south in zones following the occupation of Shuri and withdrawal of the Thirty-Second Army. The 7th Division is working with the 1st marine and 96th Division and so the dates on the map are actually reflecting movements of these forces on Okinawa. Dad's memoir reflects the dates and movements of the 7th Division which follows the aforementioned in battle. Dad's dates and the ones on the map dovetail nicely. Also, the map mentions Conical Hill. Dad is just south of Conical Hill (Gava) and moves further south in the five mile march past Yonabaru where he sets up the 7th Division machine gun. June 1st his division (as part of the 10th Army thrust) is on the move again.

machine gun emplacement but do not put the gun up until night. Our own artillery bothers us more than anything that night. The twenty-one days I am on the front lines it rains constantly. June 2, 1945 we move high on the hill and see the first real action. There are Japs killed. I help the litter bearers out. One of our boys' head is crushed, probably by machine gun bullets. That same night I move to another hill not far off where first I dig in. On June 3, 1945 I come back down in the valley with the motor section awaiting orders. Finally, we follow the rifle troops down the valley and up the mountain where I see my first dead Jap soldier. Pictures of his wife and child along with Jap money and a card, I see lying on the ground beside him. There is also a Jap machine gun site; I pick this up. Later I write home on the back of the card. *(see fig. 5-a)*

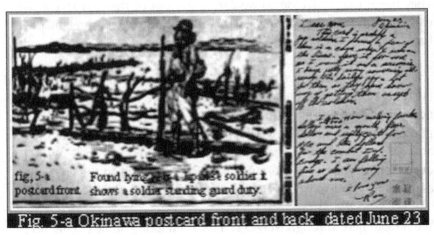

fig, 5-a Found lying by a Japanese soldier I
postcard front shows a soldier standing guard duty.

Fig. 5-a Okinawa postcard front and back dated June 23

On June 4, 1945 we leave our previous spot bright and early and make off again—always on the move! There are two Japs lying in the debris. One has a wristwatch but I am too much in a hurry to extract it. I finally reach a grassy slope that I like so I dig in for the night.

---

19 The story Dad tells originally ends here but I ask him to add just a little more since I intuit the poetic image is psychologically significantly. It is as if a flame flairs briefly and suddenly lit just prior going into the dark meat of the story unfolding ahead and this seems important on two counts, that on the level of the literary realism of the story and that on the level of the story's poetic realism. I am thinking of Gaston Bachelard's recognition in The Poetics of Space, (Beacon Press: MA, 1994 p. xv) "The poetic image is a sudden salience on the surface of the psyche."

The next day, since I am last on guard duty, I am up early. I try to build a fire; everything is very wet, it having rained last night for most of the night. My blanket is soaked.[19]

I struggle in vain to find enough dry material for a fire. A fellow soldier joins me in the search and together we do get a small fire smoldering flame started but cannot do more because of orders to leave.

It is still raining as we move out. By the time we reach our destination I am soaked to the gills. My combat boots are full of water. That night I sleep in a fox hole full of water. The only thing above water is my head, my M-1 rifle and my feet. If it were not for the mosquito repellent I am using I would be eaten alive by mosquitoes. They come down on me like dive bombers. As I glance at my watch I notice the crystal has acquired numerous cracks. Other soldiers also notice cracks in their watch crystals. We come to the conclusion it is caused by powerful repellent.

The next day, June 6, 1945, we report Japs hiding in burial tombs. Around 20:30 hours, we send up flares. One Jap is slain, another, captured. The prisoner taken is crying and yelling.

June 7th, 8th, and 9th we are in the heart of Jap territory. I pass destroyed Jap artillery pieces with many decaying enemy bodies lying around. The stench is sickening. As we move forward, sniper fire is getting too close for comfort. We have to dive into the ditch by the road side to take cover. I learn early on to watch out if I hear bullets from rifle fire "scream" and to dive for the ditch. But, if they "pop", they are over my head. Finally, we move into what is left of an Okinawan's hut and yard. After a period of time we move out and once more are under heavy sniper fire. Some of us have to go back after more ammunition. We make it alright and so all's well that ends well, as they say.

That night I pull four hours of guard duty instead of the usual two. We now expect a *banzai charge*.[20] I can hear the Japs talking. They are high on *saké* [21] and yelling "Banzai". Since we are very close, we prepare by fixing bayonets to our M-1 rifles. One Japanese yells "Banzai!" I see him rush out over a big boulder. But, just as fast he runs back to safety. It is really very intense as we expect a terrible bayonet slaughter. But, even so, it is rather comical the way it never happens.

During June 10th, 11th, and 12th we move to Chinen Peninsula and stay there the next three nights. The Japs are dug in very well. We are finding it difficult to take the peak. I fire the machine gun into burial tombs where the Japs are hiding. Tanks with flame throwers are called to fire into the tombs. This does the trick. For when the burning jelly gets on their bodies, they come out

---

20 Pronounced in English as in bone-sigh, banzai, from the Chinese "wansai" literally means 10,000 years. It is once used casually to wish long life to a person. The Emperor of China is originally addressed as Lord of Ten Thousand Years with the number denoting innumerability. The Chinese term is introduced to Japan as banzei (Kana: ばんぜい Kanji: 万歳) in the 8th century, and is used to express respect for the emperor in much the same manner as its Chinese cognate. Banzei is later revived as banzai after the Meiji Restoration. Banzai as a formal ritual is established in the promulgation of the Meiji Constitution in 1889 when university students shout banzai in front of the emperor's carriage. Around the same time, banzai comes to be used in contexts unrelated to the emperor. The supporters of the Freedom and People's Rights Movement, for example, begin to shout "Jiyu banzai" (Kanji: 自由万歳 ; Kana: じゆうばんざい, or, roughly, "Long Live Freedom!") in 1883. During WW II, banzai serves as a battle cry of sorts for Japanese soldiers. The ground troops of WWII confirm its use, heard in numerous battles during the Pacific Campaign when Japanese infantry units attack Allied positions. As a result, the term "banzai charge" (or alternatively "banzai attack") gain a common currency among English-speaking soldiers and remains the most widely understood context of the term in the West to this day. The modern use of the word among Japanese-speaking people carries a meaning similar to "hurrah" and is used to give toast at weddings wishing long life to the wedding couple and to the community gathering. It is interesting how the one word carries this double signification, both long life and immanent death. See http://en.wikipedia.org/wiki/Ten_thousand_years accessed October 21, 2013.

21 Sake or *saké* is an alcoholic beverage of Japanese origin that is made from fermented rice. Sake is sometimes referred to in English-speaking countries as "rice wine".

screaming. Those that do not burn alive surrender.[22]

I dig a comfortable hole and enjoy three good nights' sleep even though we are bothered more than ever by Jap mortar and artillery fire and also a sniper that we cannot locate. I've been in combat two weeks today, June 12, 1945, and expect to be relieved as soon as we take the peninsula. Our primary objective is not to kill Japs but to take and secure the island to prepare for our final move to take Japan and end the war. Then, we can go home.

About this time a limited supply of new fatigues are issued to soldiers whose fatigues are badly torn, muddy and dirty. Since mine only have a small hole in the right leg I am refused a new pair. I immediately put my finger in the hole and rip it all the way down to my wet, muddy, well-worn shoes. Needless to say I receive new fatigues. Since I haven't bathed for two weeks and it is not difficult to find a shell hole filled up with rain water in which to bathe, I shed all my clothes and jump in. Then, something unexpected and unlikely happens. (After all, this is the front lines and a hazardous area!) A woman and what appears to be her teenage daughter come strolling past the shell hole in which I am bathing. I think, "Will wonders never cease?" (!) The elder lady and teenage girl are looking my way and I observe the woman saying something to the girl who turns her head. But, the elderly woman continues to look as I continue to bathe. Oh well! This is war; and it sure feels good to be clean and have a new pair of fatigues!

---

22 Surrender is a new phenomenon in island warfare for the Japanese. Surrender deviates from the demands of samurai code of conduct. See Francis Trevelyn Miller, "The Battle of Okinawa, April-June 1945: War at its Worst", Salt Of America on line, article number 204. Article date 01-29-2013 , http://saltofamerica.com/contents/displayArticle.aspx?18_204 accessed October 21, 2013.

The battalion[23] supported by our Company "D" moves to the top of the escarpment at 03:30 hours. It is solid coral rock. We cannot dig holes. By way an aside, I remember lying down and putting a couple rocks near my head. I am always conscious of protecting my head. We are enduring enemy artillery fire when I hear a piece of shrapnel whizzing toward me while slowly losing momentum. The soldier next to me yells, "Ouch!" The piece of shrapnel makes a red mark on his skin but doesn't pierce it. Meanwhile, we take our objective before daylight with complete surprise to the enemy. The remainder of my day is spent in cleaning out pockets of snipers. During this time one of our men is wounded. June 13th is spent supporting the battalion in strengthening positions. Four more of our men are wounded.

By June 14th the machine gun section receives considerable knee mortar and grenade fire demonstrating how close we are to the enemy. We continue to support the battalion. Today six of our men are wounded.

On June 15th I take part in an advance of 800 yards against horrendous resistance. This moves our location up to the base of the escarpment under heavy enemy artillery fire. While I am on guard duty during the night I hear a noise behind me, one I do not expect. I flash around. Because of light from flares I can see gold teeth on dark skin. It is a Jap, or so I think. Many Japs have gold teeth. I immediately release the safety on my M-1 and am prepared to shoot when I hear a voice yell out, "It's me, Snake, don't shoot!" I never thought that "me", a mere PFC would ever bawl out a SGT. But, I surely did! Later, he and I laugh about this.

* * *

---

23 A battalion is a ground force unit composed of a headquarters with two or more companies. An officer with the rank of colonel usually commands a battalion. Company "D" is a heavy weapons company. A machine gun is considered a heavy weapon. Company "D" is one kind of company in a battalion.

THE SECRETARY OF WAR
WASHINGTON

25 May, 1945

Dear Mr. and Mrs. Van Dress:

My attention has been called
to the fact that four of your sons
are now serving in our armed forces,
and I have asked that their names be
furnished to me from the files of the
War Department, where they ap-
pear as John R. Van Dress, Troy Van
Dress, Carl G. Van Dress and Ronald
J. Van Dress all of the Army.

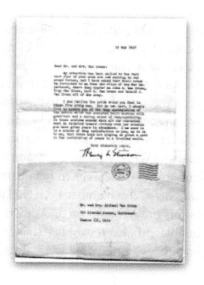

I can realize the pride which
you feel in these fine young men. For
my own part, I should like to assure
you of the deep appreciation of the nation which has accepted their
service with gratitude and a strong sense of responsibility. In these
anxious months when all our resources must be directed toward victory
over our enemies you have given yours in abundance. I am sure it is a
source of deep satisfaction to you, as it is to me, that these boys are
playing so great a part in the restoration of peace to a troubled world.

Very Truly Yours,
Henry L. Stimson

VI.

Hill 153; 7th Division June, 1945

On June 16th we move out at 03:00 hours. It is pitch black. I cannot see the man ahead of me. I can only hear his footsteps. Our objective is Hill 153. When we finally arrive at the hill it is so steep we have to use rope to reach an area where we can walk. The enemy is at the top of the hill and is using all types of weapons to keep us from reaching the top. All I can remember in my struggle to the top is a lot of noise, a lot of ammunition powder, smoke, and some men falling. When I finally do reach the tip I am summoned by three of our stretcher bearers to help carry one of our wounded soldiers to a safe area. I remember he has black curly hair. His skull is crushed; his brains are bobbing up and down as we walk and his mouth is blowing bubbles. I also remember thinking that he is alive but maybe it will have been better if he were already dead.

Our objective is taken but not without strong opposition and many casualties. On June 17th my Company "D" supports an attack with the battalion at the front until relieved by 184th infantry at 16:00 hours. Then we are going to move to bivouac area on Chinen Peninsula.

On June 18th, 1945 just before we move to bivouac area, a jeep carrying General Buckner passes us moving toward the lines. I remember wondering what he is doing in this dangerous area. It is later I learn he is slain not long after seeing him.[24] Another famous man and friend of the combat infantry soldier, Ernie Pyle, the newspaper reporter is also killed on a nearby island. Sometime later it

24 Lieut. General Simon Bolivar Buckner is killed in action June 18, 1945. See http://1-22-infantry.org/commanders/bucknerpers.htm

occurs to me I could have been General Buckner's driver. Although I am disappointed when the sergeant back in basic refuses me permission to get my military license to drive, he may have unknowingly saved my life. C'est la guerre! (That's life!)

Shortly thereafter, we reach a point where we can see the Pacific Ocean. We literally ran out of island to conquer. We are then relieved by the 184th infantry.

It is now evening June 18th. This first night in the rest area we hear three Japs coming down the cobblestone road. Our men shoot two of them; one gets away. Both Mike and I (Mike is our 2nd man on the machine gun) go down to the road and extract the belt with a buckle. It has an anchor on it. That tells us how desperate the Japanese are. They are using Navy men to do army infantry work. We have to pull the belt to get it off and it breaks. Since I have the bigger half, Mike gives me the other end of the buckle. I have the buckle on a belt to this day.

Since this is the first night off the front lines, we do not sleep in a fox hole but lay on the ground. I take my steel helmet off along with my dog tags and lay them beside me. Just before I fall asleep I hear a stone hit my helmet. I didn't know it at the time but the one Jap that gets away is trying to determine where someone is. During the night he sneaks up to where I am, takes my dog tags to pass as me and try to get through our lines. When I wake up next morning my dog tags are missing. Evidently the Jap did not attempt to take my life as I might let out a yell and he will have been captured.

We actively patrol surrounding hills and caves looking for stray Japs. Early morning on June 20th I am ordered to report to personnel. When I arrive a Personnel Sergeant identifies me and next says they shot a Jap last night who is wearing my dog tags. They are considering reporting me missing in action. He returns to me my dog tags and next informs me the real reason I am here. They are looking for a soldier who can type and my records indicate that I am that soldier they seek. A warrant officer interviews me and gives me a mental test along with a typing test. Since I pass both tests, he says to me, "Effective immediately you are now on duty with Personnel. You are Company clerk for Co. "D" 17th Inf. 7th Division." (See Letter To Mom dated June 20, 1945) Although I do not want to leave my outfit, I know our next combat would be Japan and I realize it will be a lot easier on Mom if I can tell her I now have a less dangerous assignment. It is just after a couple days of orientation on June 22nd that I begin my regular administrative duties at Personnel.

On June 19th Japanese general, General Ushijima gives orders to resist to the very end. On June 20-21 nearly four thousand Japanese and conscripted Okinawans surrender. June 21, 1945 our 7th division captures the hill of General Ushijima's headquarters cave. On June 22-23 General Mituru Ushijima, commander of Japan's 32nd Army and Chief of Staff, Isamu Cho commit *seppuku*.[25]

* * *

---

25 Literally, 'stomach-cutting", *seppuku* is ritual suicide by disembowelment. Part of the samurai bushido honor code, seppuku is originally reserved for samurai to die with honor rather than fall into the hands of their enemies. The Japanese reading is hara-kiri, which means the same thing, "cutting the belly". It is my understanding the term *seppuku* is used when writing whereas hara-kiri is the spoken word, the word one uses when talking about the act of ritual suicide.

LETTERS TO MOM

June 18, 1945

Okinawa

My Dearest Mother,

You were probably worrying since I haven't written to you for quite some time, and you have probably guessed the reason why. I have been on the front lines for twenty-one days; we were relieved yesterday. I am now safe and sound in a rest camp writing to the one I love most.

While I was on the lines I received all your back mail and also your present mail up to June 4th and which I got yesterday and don't you think I didn't have time to read them for we always have time to read our mail. In fact, I read these twice. There were approximately fifteen letters in all. Dorothy and Carl's letters were also appreciated. I will write to Carl immediately.

I got all the stamps you sent and also the pictures of Jean

Malloy and her husband.

You asked me a lot of questions which I would answer but since they were in the older letters I received from you it won't be necessary as you already know them.

Mother I save all your letters, but I am getting too many of them now and it's pretty hard to carry them around. Would you want me to destroy them or send them home to you?

I have found a lot of souvenirs up on the front; a Jap belt which I am wearing, site off of a Jap machine gun, an opium pipe and some real Jap money which I will enclose in this letter—three bills.

Well, Mother, since I receive your letters regularly now ask me anything you want to know and I will answer your questions.

photo: three Japanese bills accompanying letter 18 June, 1945

June 20, 1945

Okinawa

Dear Mother,

      I received another letter dated June 7th. It is swell that Troy gets to come home so often especially since Dorothy is in her present condition. Did Troy say that president Truman is a good worker?

      Is it possible that John might be coming home as I believe it is doubtful that he would be moved to another island after being on new Caledonia for so long.

      Mother, co. [company]*[26] clerk has gone to the hospital, so they called me for an interview yesterday, gave me a few tests, which I passed—hence, I am now going to be the co, clerk.

      I hesitated when they offered the position to me as there are rumors that we might not enter combat for another six months since the battle here on Okinawa is almost at an end, and I have made such good friends here. But, then I knew that if I got the job, your mind would be greatly relieved since a co. clerk doesn't go into battle. I hope you will cease all your worrying about me now, as I can tell by your letters you are doing too much of it.

Love,

Ronnie

---
26 *editor's insertion

51

VII.

The War Ends

On July 2, 1945 General Joseph Stilwell, Buckner's replacement, announces the campaign is officially over. On August 6, 1945 an atomic bomb is dropped on Hiroshima and three days later, on August 9, 1945, an atomic bomb is dropped on Nagasaki. This is followed by surrender of Emperor Hirohito August 15, 1945.

I am lying on my bunk when I hear the news. The war is over. We will not have to fight another battle in Japan. Happy Days! All hell breaks loose. Soldiers are so happy they begin firing all kinds of weapons. I think to myself how ironic it would be to make it through battle without a scratch only to get hit with a stray bullet now. I get down on the ground under my bunk and I do not get up until the rejoicing is over.

On September 8, 1945 we arrive at Inch'ong Bay, Korea, drop anchor and disembark. During this moment I cannot keep from thinking I have as much voyage time as some of the sailors on board the ship.

VIII.

Korea

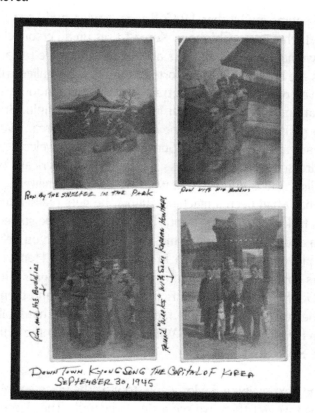

Ron by the shelter in the park
Ron with his buddies
Ron and his buddies
Ramsd "weeds" with some Korean Heathen
Downtown Kyongsong the Capital of Korea
September 30, 1945

On September 9th we motor convoy out ten miles and arrive at Taejon-ni. We set up our office in a factory building. One September 14th we leave Taejon-ni by motor convoy and drive twenty miles to Kyonsong, the capital of Korea. We set up office in the Japanese 78th Regiment Barrack area. On September 16th I am finally able to write home on some Japanese stationary I find in the barracks area. (See the following photo collage of the original letter and envelope in the

53

"Letters To Mom" section at the close of this chapter.)

On September 30, 1945 I go on pass with some friends to downtown Kyonsong. While the pictures I include to accompany this memoir did not come out well, they do show the architecture present in the capital city during the 1940's. (Also see the September 30th letter to my mother reporting my adventures.)

Sometime in October 1945 Briggs, Saylor, and I are sent on advance detachment to Ch'ohgju, Korea to set up a Personnel Office. Although we have First Class seats aboard the train, the remainder of the cars are crowded with all sorts of materials and filled with people—even on the roofs of the train. After several hours we reach our destination. Our second night in downtown Ch'ongju, Briggs and I decide to go into town to become familiar with the area. We stop at what appears to be a nightclub. Some business men welcome us inside. One well-dressed man in a business suit much like Americans wear can speak English. He is interested in what we do in the military. When I tell him that I had been a machine gunner, he gets really interested and wants to know all about it, but I keep changing the subject and he catches on and orders American music played. Would you believe the first song played is "I'll Be Down To Get You In A Taxi Honey"? He then orders some hot saké and introduces us to some girls who are evidently Geisha.[27] The one wants to dance with me and then feed me which is the custom but the only food I recognize is a hardboiled egg. We end up having a good time. When we get back to the office we tell our friend, Saylor all about it.

The next evening Saylor wants to visit the place so we all go back. When we get there we see a sign is posted. The sign reads, "Off Limits". Before we know it an MP[28] drives up in a jeep and demands to know what we are doing here. He takes our name, rank and serial number. We think we are really in trouble but hear no more about this.

---

27 Geisha references a Japanese hostess trained to entertain men with conversation, dance and song.

28 Military police

Some weeks later, after the rest of the personnel staff join us we are busy working the morning report section when the same MP enters the office. We think for sure he comes to report on us. About half an hour he leaves and we never hear another word about that episode. C'est la vie![29]

Shortly thereafter three Japanese interpreters are assigned to a private room off of our sleeping quarters. The main interpreter is a former captain in the Japanese Army during the war. After the war he is discharged and subsequently he is hired as an interpreter for the 7th Division. He is fluent in Japanese, Korean, and English. He and I become quite friendly. He explains to me Japanese soldiers are beaten for violations. He says he is beaten as a soldier and beat other soldiers of lesser rank. I have him write in Japanese the name of the street in the picture of a typical street scene in downtown Ch'ongju, Korea. He also runs errands for me like purchasing eggs. Eggs are a real treat for me since I have not had them for so long. In fact, one of my "Letters To Mom" is all about having two fried eggs. At this time it occurs to me how the Japanese interpreter and I are friendly now but a few short months ago we are mortal enemies.

---

29 French phrase for "It is life" or "Such is life" or simply "That's life". The phrase means life is what it is.

top: "Just for Fun" bottom left: Leading Local Military, Ron and Briggs Chongju 1946 bottom cntr: W Vick, R Briggs, Korean gal & baby on her back and Ron   top rt: "a Street Scene" Chongju, Korea, 1946 second rt: "The Crew", Personnel Office Staff third rt: "Atop the Howitzer", Ron & crew bottom rt: Willis Vick pulling Ron in rickshaw

In combat most military protocol is dispensed. Proper military uniform is not an issue. However, I continue to wear the Japanese belt with the Navy buckle in Korea now. My captain, Captain Brenner, our Personnel Officer, is a stickler for proper military dress and somewhat priggish—a "stuffed shirt". He informs his Warrant Officer to have me remove the offensive belt and replace it with the regulation military belt.

I am serving as company clerk since June 20th, 1945. This position calls for the rank of T-5 or corporal and merits higher pay. I am still a PFC. Maybe because of this incident Captain Brenner delays my promotion. Shortly thereafter, Captain Brenner is replaced by 1st Lt. Roger K Hamilton. He wonders why I am company clerk for so long and never promoted. After investigating he immediately promotes me to corporal.

As time goes by[30] we begin wondering what we are doing

here. Russia is occupying the northern half of the 38th parallel. We are occupying the southern half. The war in Europe is over for some time and the last battle of the Pacific, The Battle of Okinawa is won. Hirohito surrenders on August 15, 1945. No one wants to hear about the world war anymore. Time is becoming "hum-drum" and lax. The food is lousy, usually stale biscuits with canned vegetables. I start to desire C-rations like the kind I get on the front lines. We try to rob the mess hall storage room; there is nothing here but canned cheese. Soldiers start writing home about how bad things are. Parents begin complaining to Congressmen. Investigations are conducted and rumor has it the Black Market is taking liberty with the food supply. After a few months food and mail suddenly return to normal.

CHONGJU KOREA — 1946 —

PERSONNEL OFFICE STAFF

TYPICAL STREET SCENE IN CHONGJU KOREA

To pass the time I become almost professional at table tennis and a pretty good 2nd baseman or shortstop on the softball team.

30 It is currently 1946, probably early spring.

During the period mail delivery is so bad and Mom does not hear from me for several weeks (or maybe longer due to a little negligence on my part); she asks my brother, Troy, who works at the Pentagon, to investigate. I include the letter I subsequently receive from Personnel and immediately answer.[31]

***

---

31 The letter referenced is written on the back of the official letter from Personnel dated March 30, 1946 demanding this soldier write his mother.

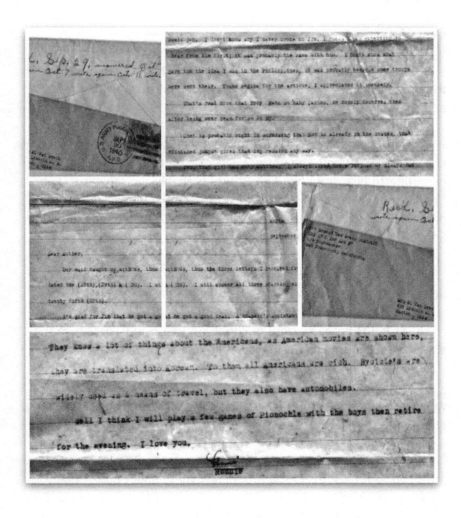

Korea

September 16, 1945

Dear Mother,

Our mail caught up with us; thus the three letters I received
from you dated the (25th), (29th) & (30). I will answer all three
starting with the twenty-fifth (25th).

I'm glad for Jim that he got a good deal. A Chaplin's Assistant
is a swell job. I don't know why I never wrote to Jim, I guess I was
expecting to hear from him first; it was probably the same with him.
I don't know what gave him the idea I was in the Philippines, it was
probably because some troops were sent there. Thank Regina for the
article, I appreciated it immensely.

That's real nice that Troy gets so many passes, he surely
deserves them after being overseas so long.

Chet is probably right in surmising that Bob is already in the
states, that "finished jumps" gives that impression any way.

Yes, that girl was Ruby Matthews; I always liked her a lot, as
we always had a lot of fun talking together. If you see her again, Pop,
tell her I said hello.

I have already peered into the college situation. In fact, I was
attracted to it back in Hawaii. As things stand now I have already
made up my mind to take advantage of it. I plan to take a course for
announcing. But then, I have also thought that once I get back home,
I will want to stay there for a good long time. No, I don't think that

Red Cross idea will work out, but you do anything you please, as anything that satisfies you, goes double with me. As for supporting you, I want that to be solely my responsibility when I come home, for the rest of our lives. You may not know it but you and your prayers have pulled me through many a crisis a few months ago and that I will never forget.

No, I have not discontinued my war bonds yet, but I plan to do so soon. The reason you haven't been getting them is the fact that they make them out only when our payroll comes out. I did not get paid from the time I left Saipan until after the Battle for Okinawa was over. As I have told you in a previous letter, I have a hundred  and fifty (150.00) dollars on the way home. My bonds will probably arrive at the same time.

The last time I wrote you I was in a building that was part warehouse, hospital, and administrative. I lived in the administrative section. Well, we moved several days ago to the capital. (Kyongsong) We took over buildings that the Japs used when they were here.

The Koreans seem to like us pretty well; I have learned a few sentences in Korean which I use constantly to converse with them. The GI's have already started to whistle at the women here. They are very modest, blush a little and walk on. They know a lot of things about Americans; as American movies are shown here, they are translated into Korean. To them all Americans are rich. Bicycles are widely used as a means of travel but they also have automobiles.

Well, I think I will play a few games of Pinochle with the boys then retire for the evening. I love you.

Ronnie

P.S.

Enclosed is clipping.
Say hello to Auseon's and Dorothy for me.

~

Kyongsong, Korea

September 30, 45

Mother Dear,

They finally released passes Monday the twenty fourth (24th) thus it was possible for me to get one Wednesday. I really enjoyed myself. I will tell you about it.

First I should relay to you that I almost have a private room (my sleeping quarters) only two other boys are in it; they both work at Personnel with me. The one boy, Briggs, whom I believe I mentioned in a previous letter, went on pass with me. Well to go on, Briggs and myself awakened approximately seven thirty, (7:30), our usual time, had breakfast, washed, etc. and about nine o'clock (9) found ourselves walking up the avenue of everyday life to the Koreans, but adventure to us.

It was about a half-hour walk to the main part of Kyongsong, but we were there before we knew it. Along the way I gave a kid about twelve (12) years old a stick of chewing gum and a candy bar. The Koreans just love American cigarettes, chewing gum, and candy. I should say they love Americans. So as a result I could not get rid of him for some time.

Everywhere you look there are signs saying "Welcome Americans" and "American Liberators of Korea Welcome". Even the movies are free to GI's; they only cost three (3) yen, about twelve and a half (12½) cents in American money. At first we could not find a theater so I, having my English Korean Phrase Book with me, of course, tried my best to make one of the populace understand me. Briggs and I finally got our lingo across so we hired rickshaws—you know what they are, somewhat of a buggy pulled by a man instead of a horse. As a result we went to a movie just as the wealthier Koreans do. We did not stay in the movie but ten minutes (10) as it was somewhat stuffy and not very good anyway. After that we walked the streets peering at all the more interesting sights until we came to a bar. It had Korean writing on the front and above it were the words, "Bar Come Back" written in English. We sauntered in, looked the place over and were ready to go when I spied one of the boy waiters with a pretty nice wrist watch. Well, I tried my best to give him a sales talk, but not without provocations; it was useless as he was definitely convinced to keep his watch. But, I have learned not to give up things that easy so I sat at one of the vacant tables and continued making certain offers for his watch. No sooner did I sit down when a very pretty Korean girl asked me what I wished to drink. Saki being the common drink over here, I ordered some. She was back in a couple minutes, poured my drink then nonchalantly sat on my lap. I did not know what to expect until I found out that this was the custom and she was the so-called Geisha girl. People back in the States have the wrong impression of these girls; they are not exactly bad but rather, educated entertainers. A Geisha has to go to college. Most of them go to a college in Tokyo; they know how to sing and dance and are good conversationalists— practically everything along those lines. Very shortly she made a motion to the bartender. Music filled the room and we were dancing. She was very short, about five feet, I should say, and to my surprise,

63

she followed me very well. She was very interesting, always sitting on my lap and occasionally she sang Japanese songs to me. You know how they go, Mom, somewhat like a death chant; you've heard them on the radio. It was all very amusing and something to remember. She could say several English phrases; one of them was "I love you." After we were together for some time, she whispered this to me. That's when I pulled out a few pictures I have and showed them to her. I pointed out the picture of you and me explaining to her that you were my Mother, then I showed her a picture I have of another girl and told her it was my girlfriend. She made a remark about her blond hair and about our home. To her it was a mansion as the homes over here don't even compare to our cellar. After that I told Briggs that it was getting pretty late and if we wanted to get some souvenirs, we had better leave. He agreed. So I gave this girl a couple sticks of chewing gum, which as I explained before is a novelty here, and we were on our way again.

I bought several articles; one is an oriental doll that I will send home as soon as possible. I also have some handkerchiefs which I will enclose in this letter. You can give one to Dolores, Eve and Regina, if you wish.

By the way, Michael, I happened to get a Japanese rifle. It's a little beat up; probably been through the last war and this one, too. But, I thought you would like it anyway. How about that?

Well I sort of interrupted my adventures, didn't I? As you know, they are not quite over yet. I am now walking down Jun Gung Street (or some sort of name similar to that) when I am confronted by someone who says he is a Korean guide. I had all intentions of telling you this one, Mom, but it's getting pretty late and I want to answer some questions you asked in your letter. I will tell you the above adventure when we are together.

When I returned from pass that evening I found two letters from you and *The Commodore*[*32] from Dolores lying on my desk, which I appreciated very much. Thank you for the news, Dolores.

Yes, I am in the Tenth Army and approximately one hundred miles (100) from Jim. Yokahama is in Japan, you know, not too far from Tokyo. The Sea of Japan separates Korea from the coast of Japan.

About that check; I knew it was a hundred and fifty two dollars (152.00) but I just gave the round figures to you.

Bo also sent me a picture of Dolores Gartner; also one of Veronica Titta. It won't be long now till practically everyone in our room is engaged or married.

Thank you very much for thinking of me, Pat and Donna. A big kiss and hug for both of you and don't wipe the kisses off either. Have a good time at the party.

It must be late as Briggs is sleeping on a couple of office chairs, so I will close for now.

I love you,

Ronnie

32 *Editor's Note: The Commodore is a 1945 local publication through The Commodore Barry Club, St John High School, Canton, Ohio.

SAVE

WAR DEPARTMENT
THE ADJUTANT GENERAL'S OFFICE
WASHINGTON 25, D.C.

REPLY TO AGPB-I 201 Van Dress, Ronald J.   Vieca

(9 Feb 46)   30 March 1946

Subject: Advise soldier to write.

To: Commanding Officer
        17th Infantry
        APO 7, c/o Postmaster
        San Francisco, California

        1. It is requested that the soldier named below be advised
to write to his mother, Mrs. M. Van Dress, 516 Lincoln Avenue,
Northwest, Canton, Ohio.

        2. The latest report received in this office relative to
this soldier's whereabouts is shown as follows: 27 March 1946
Radio shows Ronald J. Van Dress, #35850415, a Corporal, Company D,
17th Infantry, APO 7, c/o Postmaster, San Francisco, California.

Dear Mom,
        Here is the correspondence we received here at Personnel in regards to
Troys inquiry. Below is how it would be answered then forwarded to Washington
D. C. if I would'nt work here.

                        By order of the Secretary of War:

                                                        Adjutant General.
201-Van Dress, Ronald J.   1st Ind   RKR/rjv

            Compliance to basic communications has been complied
    with.

                                        ROGER K. HAMILTON
                                        1st Lt., Infantry
                                        PERSONNEL ADJUTANT

Turn to the other side for my letter.

Ch'ongju, Korea

April 11, 1946

Dear Mom,

Potatoe salad, baked beans, and boiled wieners…that was one of my favorite meals when I was home and the mention of the aroma of pumpkin pie started my tape worm to squirming.

I'll bet the bedroom will look swell in peach and chenille rugs; I didn't know you had them.

Well, it won't be long before Carl will be popping in the front door and I can imagine your anxiety as well as the thrill he will get after being away for so long.

By your letter of 27 March, '46 which, incidentally, took almost two weeks to get here—and I reiterate the word incidentally when I say that is very good time. (I think the reason for the fast delivery now is due to the fact that so many families wrote the War Dept. concerning the mail situation.) As I was saying… "by your letter of 27 March, '46", as well as

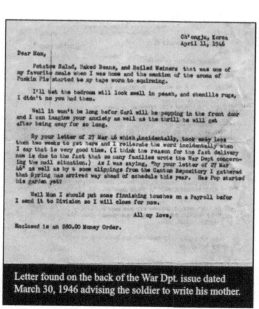

Letter found on the back of the War Dpt. issue dated March 30, 1946 advising the soldier to write his mother.

by some clippings from the Canton Repository, I gathered that spring has arrived way ahead of schedule this year. Has Pop started his garden yet?

Well Mom I should put some finishing touches on a payroll before I send it to Division so I will close for now.

All my love,

Enclosed is an $80.00 money order.

~

IX.

"A Real Happy Guy"

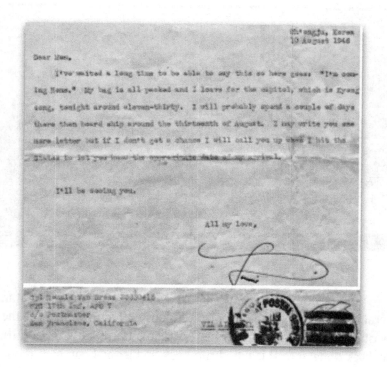

Well…Finally!

     I receive the good word and for it see the letter to my mom dated August 10, 1946, for it tells it best. Also see the letter from Yung Dung Poe, Korea dated August 15, 1946; and if you want to see a really happy guy, see the picture of me waiting with barracks bags full of gear for the ship that will bring me to the states. The ship is The Sea Star.

Going Home

"A Really Happy Guy"

On or about Saturday, August 17th we board The Sea Star. Several days later the sea becomes "choppy". I am standing at the bow of the ship when the sea opens up like a bottomless pit and the bow dives down into this pit. I run back as fast as I can just as sea water covers the deck. The order is given that everyone must go below deck into the hold. I am the last soldier to go below. I am terribly sea sick.

It appears that everyone is. I manage to get one soda cracker. It must have taken me an hour to consume it with the tip of my tongue. I finally feel better but the ship is creaking and groaning. For thirty-six crucial hours we pass through a sample of that peculiar weather phenomenon called by our late enemies, the Japanese, a

70

Kamikaze[33] or *Divine Wind*. It is called by those same people, *taifun*. It is from the Japanese the word typhoon comes to the American language. Is this the last disaster to keep us from getting home? Or is there more to come? To quote our ship's transport chaplain, C.H. Harris, "We can count ourselves fortunate that our experience lasts but little better than one day and night." Yes, thank God there is no loss of human life and no serious injuries.

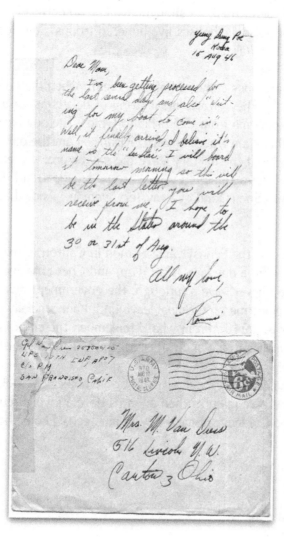

---

33 神 kami means "god" and "divine" + 風 kaze "wind"

Sometime in September, on a very foggy morning we see the Golden Gate Bridge in California. We disembark. The next ten days are spent processing. The final step is financial to the tune of $300, mustering out pay. Everyone is sailing right through the line until it comes to me. There is a mistake in my financial records that cannot be corrected until tomorrow. "This can't be," I think. "Tomorrow is eternity; the government can keep the money; I am going home!" But, no way! And then I think, "I should have known better!" I am put in a room that normally houses five hundred troops...all alone. I feel dejected and demoralized.

Morning does come. I hold my breath when they process me. I finally make it. They give to me a string of tickets about a yard long that will transport me from California to Ohio. The one nice thing from it all is that I am traveling with civilians. I am the only military man aboard. All of the military leave the day before. I even get to sit next to and get acquainted with a pretty American girl, the first in over two years. She is kind of a mystery woman. And, that is a whole other story.

I arrive at the Pennsylvania Station in Canton, Ohio about 10:30 p.m.. I am a day late. Carl, Pop, and Chet Shindler are waiting for me. Since I never have a furlough, the government owes me time; and so, they place me on terminal leave until I am officially discharged on November 8, 1946. From what I remember, the city of Canton seems a lot smaller to me and rather desolate at this time of night.

Mom is waiting for me when I arrive home. We hold onto each other for about five minutes then all of us have a joyous reunion with coffee and food. I leave home a boy of nineteen. I come home a man of 21.

All's well that ends well.

EPILOGUE

In World War I they call it shell shocked. In the beginning of World War II it is called battle fatigue. It is now called post-traumatic stress disorder (PTSD).

Whatever the name, PTSD in wartime is due to the terrific strain and horrendous conditions soldiers face in combat. It can happen while in combat or not show up until many months later.

The repeated scream of artillery shells, the throb of mortar fire, the rat-a-tat-tat of machinegun fire, the flying shrapnel from grenades, the pop of small arms bullets overhead from M-1 and carbines, needless to say cause stress to the best soldier.

Then, there is the sight of carrying a soldier to safety knowing he has a fractured skull and his brains are hanging out and seeing and hearing human beings screaming after being sprayed with napalm, a highly inflammable, jelly-like substance. Such things leave a lasting impression on soldiers. No wonder some combat soldiers wake-up from a sound sleep screaming and soaking wet with perspiration.

It's inhuman…war. War is really hell. It should be banned for all eternity. It takes years for a combat soldier to overcome the effects and stress of battle.

Even if he overcomes the stress, the scar remains.

RJ Van Dress
April, 2015

ABOUT THE AUTHOR

After WWII RJ Van Dress returns to Canton, Ohio to work briefly in radio for the Canton, "Wand", and attend Kent State University where he meets and marries the pretty girl sitting next to him in French class. Together for 66 years this August 17, 2015, RJ Van Dress and his wife, Caroline Uhl Van Dress reside in a Victorian home that sits upon seven acres in Maximo, Ohio, a little town between Canton and Akron, Ohio. Over the many years the couple works together to restore their home in original grandeur. Their home currently lists on the National Register of Historic Buildings.

Over the first fifteen years after WWII RJ Van Dress works for the Department of the Army and is made an honorary member of "The Red Devils" before transferring to the Department of Agriculture Field Office of the Food and Nutrition Service. As Officer-In Charge he opens and administers "The Food Stamp Program" and does "School Lunch Reviews". He retires at age 52 for several years before taking a new position of Director-Counselor of The Western Mahoning County Community Action Center located in Sebring, Ohio. He spends many fruitful years helping the poor and disabled before permanently retiring at the age of sixty-five. This July, he celebrates turning ninety.

Over the years RJ's avocation is raising fruits and vegetables. He and his wife farm a portion of their seven acres still. His wife Caroline writes of him,

Continued

"He loves the garden and is gratified when he produces the finest quality vegetables for our table. He also makes bread, very good bread and if that is not enough, he is good at competitive sports like baseball; he ice skates well and is a good dancer. I am not a good dancer but when we dance together, he makes me look like I am."

Furthermore, she writes, "he is gifted with a good voice and the ability to sway an audience. He can read aloud and entertain you like you are a child and your Dad is reading you a story. Although to hear him tell it he is only "talking", after 66 years together I would still rather talk with him than any other person I know."

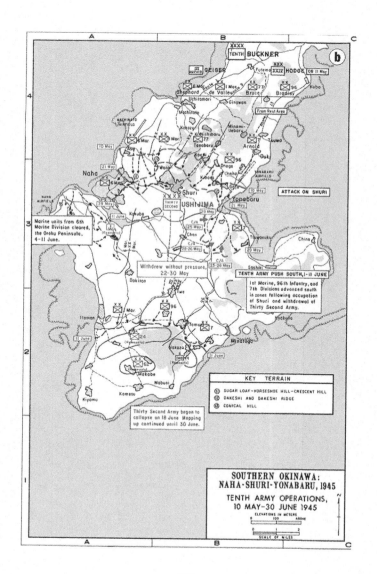

Made in the USA
Las Vegas, NV
06 December 2023

82233783R00056